ordinary
terrible
things

Forever and Ever

Dearly Beloved

Death Is Stupid

written and illustrated by Anastasia Higginbotham

AT THE CITY UNIVERSITY OF NEW YORK
NEW YORK CITY

Published in 2016 by the Feminist Press
at the City University of New York
The Graduate Center
365 Fifth Avenue, Suite 5406
New York, NY 10016

feministpress.org

First printing April 2016

Illustration and design by Anastasia Higginbotham
Photography by Alexa Hoyer
Production by Drew Stevens and Suki Boynton

Special thanks to Lionel Luongo Higginbotham for his careful editing and guidance.

Library of Congress Cataloging-in-Publication Data is available for this title.

Manufactured by Thomson-Shore, Dexter, MI, USA; RMA95HS74, December, 2015

for my FATHER 1938 –

who loses it at funerals

and my

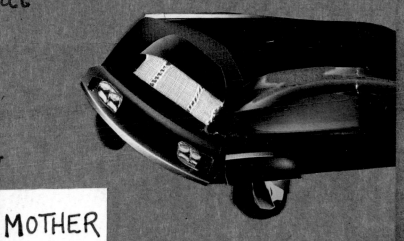

MOTHER 1941 –

who trusts that all will be well

When a loved one dies

5

people can say some....

Don't cry.
Just be grateful for the time you had with her.
...stupid things.

Even the people who care
about you most
        may not know
        what to say.

Every life comes to an end.

Dying is not a punishment.

Heavens NO!

But it mostly doesn't feel fair.

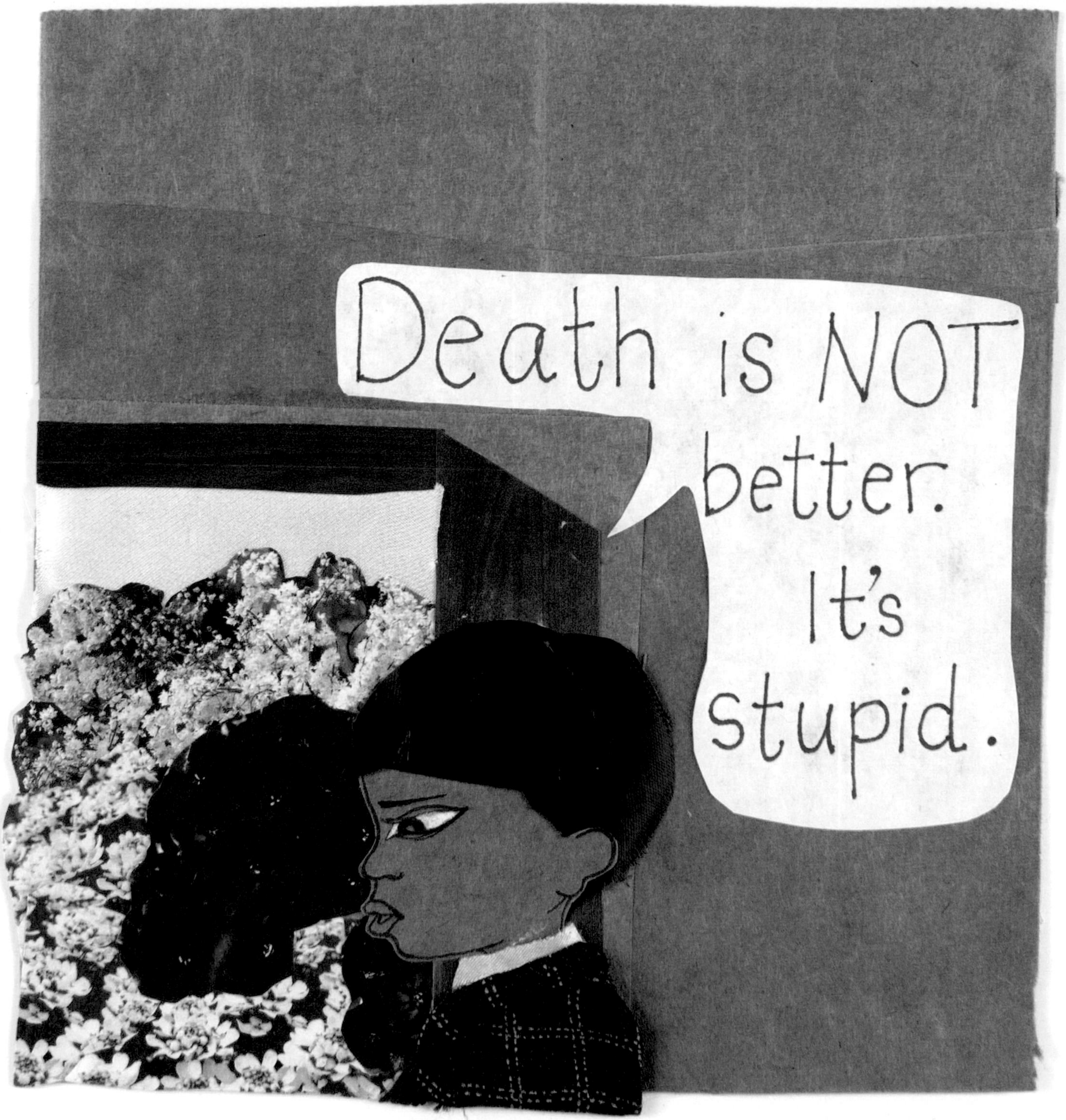
Death is NOT better. It's stupid.

Some people may try to help
and make it worse.

21

Beliefs

about what happens after death are personal to each of us. We ALL have our own ways of understanding (and NOT understanding) this mystery. Search your ❤ and other sources you trust to find out what you believe.

But beware of the lies.

She's only sleeping.

Don't say that to me.
Sleep is what I do and I wake up every morning.

It takes courage to go on living...

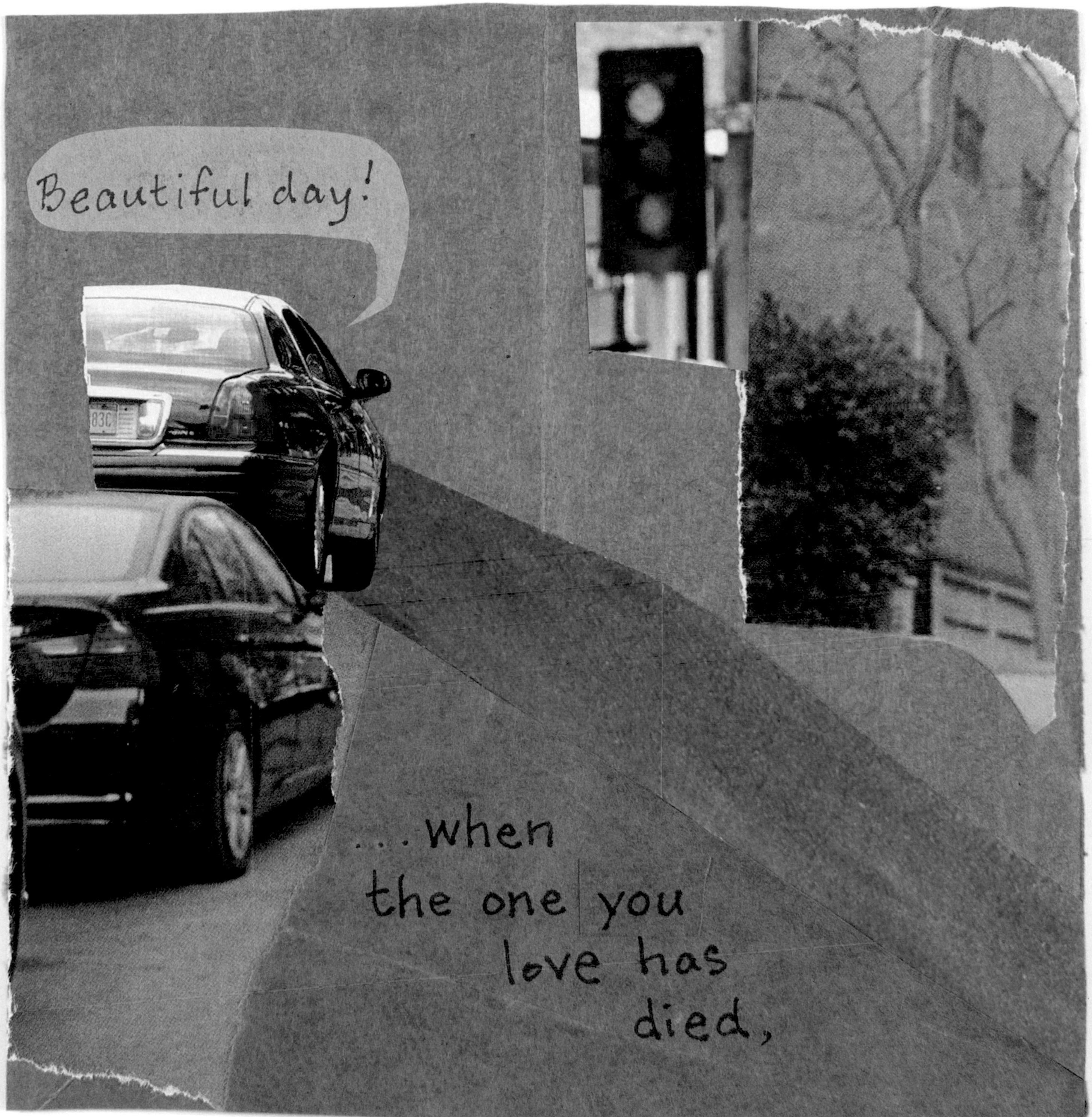
Beautiful day!
...when the one you love has died,

and to
accept that
death
cannot be
changed.

29

Everyone eventually has an
experience of someone
who died.

a member of their family

a good friend

someone they thought

would live a lot longer

We did
everything
we could.

I'm sorry.

Your pain is not
less than theirs.
It's not more.

It's not the same.

by the grief of those you depend on.

My dad cried at the
funeral. Not the
quiet Kind of crying—
it was the Kind
you can hear.

If you have
questions
for the one
who died,
ask them

...in your imagination

or
right
out
loud.

43

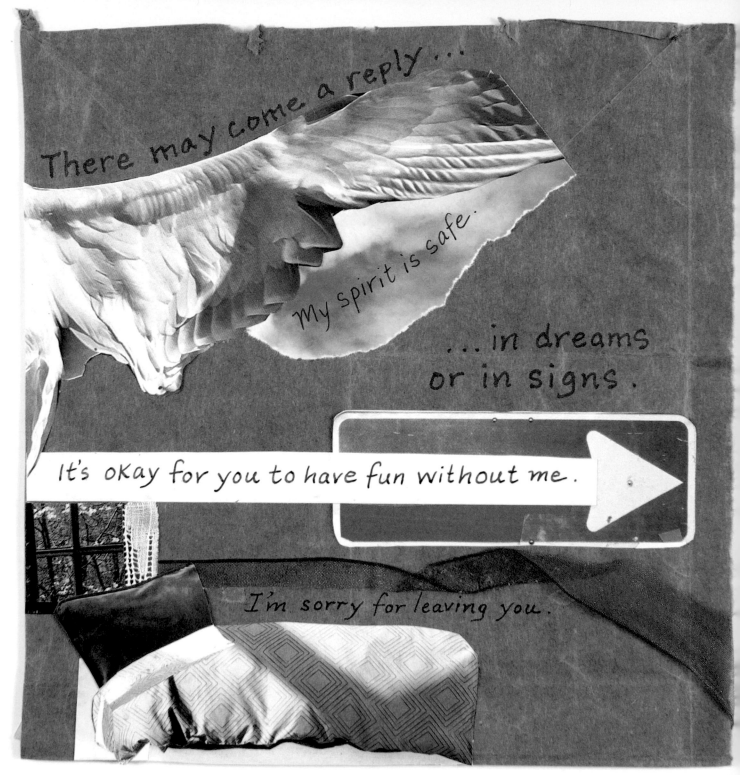

Let's get you dressed.

But we do get to remember them

long after their lives
have ended.

These connections make death less Scary and they make life more fun.

stupid

the end

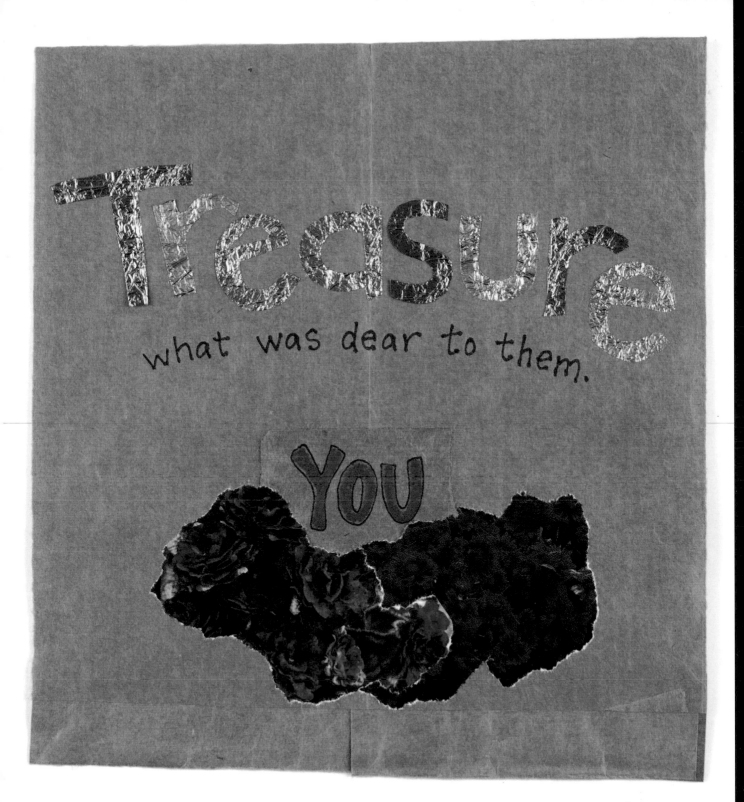

Treasure

what was dear to them.

You

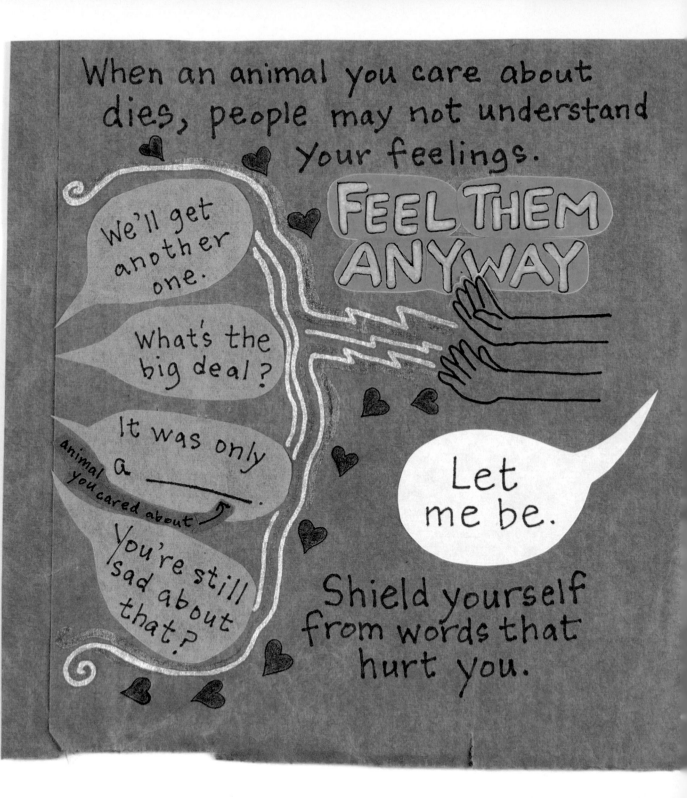

Here is a place for the name or picture of

an animal or maybe more than 1

Hey. You can hold a ceremony for a pet! Play a song. Plant a plant.

Say their name.

whom you will remember always

Names are magical. They are like spells.

NONNO

Think of the name of the one you love who has died.

Picture it in ribbons, in sequins, in paper, in string.

MAMIE

Silver pen.
Gold pen.
Googly eyes.
Crayon.

Notice how it feels to

see it

hear it

...say it

make it

Connie Bo Dean

KATHY

Jidu

TONY

Ethel Lee

Sandra

George + Anita

63

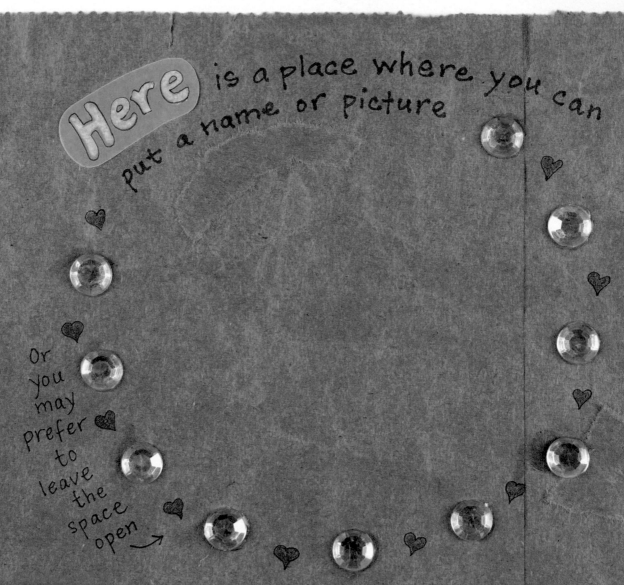

Here is a place where you can put a name or picture

Or you may prefer to leave the space open →

This is one small way to connect with your feelings and keep the one you care for — and it is enough.

Anastasia Higginbotham's books about ordinary, terrible things tell stories of children who navigate trouble with their senses sharp and souls intact.

Help may come from family, counselors, teachers, and dreams — but it's the children who find their own way through.

Anastasia has been making books by hand her whole life as a way to cope with change and grow.

‐ You CAN TOO! ‐

ordinary
terrible
things

ordinary
terrible
things